MW00986264

Outsider's Guide

to

Orthodox Judaism

by

Rabbi Arnie Singer

The Outsider's Guide to Orthodox Judaism
First Edition
Copyright © 2008 by Arnold Singer
All rights reserved.
This book may not be reproduced in whole or in part, by any means, without permission.

Rabbi Arnie Singer
arnie.singer@gmail.com
www.arniesinger.com
212-663-9550

To my loving parents,
Marc and Jeane Singer
For giving me the gift of a Jewish
education.

To Natalie,
For giving me the strength and
encouragement
to continue growing.

Table of Contents

Life-cycle

Holidays

Appendix

INTRODUCTION

Before becoming a rabbi, I worked in the corporate and business worlds for many years. As an Orthodox Jew, I was regularly called upon to explain why I did or didn't do or believe certain things, by my non Jewish or non Orthodox friends and colleagues. Although I appreciated their sincere curiosity and thirst for knowledge, I often felt uncomfortable discussing religion in the workplace. I also didn't want to serve as the spokesman for worldwide Orthodox Judaism. Who wants that kind of pressure? I just wanted to be treated like everyone else and go unnoticed.

If there had only been a guidebook that I could have given them that would answer their questions and explain the basics of Orthodox Judaism, how much easier and less stressed would my life have been? Well, there wasn't, so I decided to write *The Outsiders Guide to Orthodox Judaism,* in which I explain the fundamental Orthodox Jewish beliefs and practices in a concise and practical manner to make it possible for "outsiders" to better understand their Orthodox friends, employees, or coworkers. My intention is not to defend Orthodoxy, prove its validity, or preach its observance. It is just to describe its beliefs and practices to those unfamiliar with them.

The Outsider's Guide to Orthodox Judaism is divided into four sections. The first section summarizes fundamental beliefs including God, the soul, and the Messiah. The second section summarizes basic practices that might be encountered when interacting with Orthodox Jews including the Sabbath, kosher rules, and prayer. There are also chapters describing clothing, etiquette, and appearance. The third section explains the major life-cycle events, from birth to death. The fourth section describes each of the holidays and the rules associated with them. The appendix has charts and lists, for quick reference.

Regarding beliefs, there is not just one right way that is accepted by all segments of the Orthodox community. There are differences of opinion among Orthodox rabbis and scholars. In some cases I have presented dissenting opinions, but in most, I have written what I feel to be correct and acceptable to a majority of the community.

Regarding practices, there are also many different acceptable ways of observance. I have tried to present those that take into account the most stringent practitioner. If you see someone doing less, it doesn't mean that they are wrong. It doesn't mean that they're right either. As the saying goes, "don't judge Judaism by the Jews."

Here are a few things you should know while reading this book:

The information in this edition refers primarily to the Orthodox community in America. Israeli orthodoxy differs in certain ways and requires a separate guidebook.

The Orthodox community in America can be divided into three broad segments: Modern Orthodox, Ultra Orthodox, and Chassidic. Within each of these there are subsegments with slight variations, but I have focused only on the main ones just mentioned. The differences between these three main segments primarily relate to the "practices" section. Almost no differences exist regarding beliefs, life-cycle, and holidays. There are two accepted ways of pronouncing certain sounds in hebrew. I have chosen the one that is more popular in the Orthodox community in America.

Beliefs

GOD

It is impossible to understand or describe the essence of God. God can only be fathomed by describing what God is not, and how God relates to the world.

1. God is not human and has no body, form, or gender. It is customary to refer to God as He, but the pronoun She could very well be used since, as we just said, God is beyond the realm of gender. In fact, there are instances in the prayer liturgy that refer to God in the feminine form. This is because, according to the mystical teachings, there are both feminine and masculine attributes in the world. Anything that is proactive or aggressive is considered to be masculine, and anything that receives, accepts, or is passive is considered feminine. These attributes, or forces, manifest themselves in the human reproductive anatomy, where man gives and woman receives and nurtures. God is referred to in either the feminine or masculine form, depending on how He is perceived to relate

to, or interact with, the world. Any further explanation of this concept is beyond the scope of this book. In the interest of keeping the text uniform, I will refer to God only in the masculine form.

2. God is not bound by time. He has no beginning or end. He is infinite. Imagine outer space. Is there a point at which it ends? If you keep going will you eventually fall off? Think about it for a moment. This is infinity. There is no beginning or end. Now apply this to your understanding of God. There is no past, present, or future for God. Therefore, He cannot make mistakes or change His mind. However, God can present Himself to the world as being bound by the rules of time, so as to make it possible to relate to Him. This explains the many instances in the bible where God is portrayed as changing His mind, remembering, forgetting, or asking questions. Within the time-bound restrictions of the world, God gives Man the free will to lead his life in the way he chooses. Since God exists beyond time, the past, present, and future of His creation is revealed in it's entirety before Him.

3. God is not bound by space. God is not confined to a building, or to a geographic region, or to a place referred to as heaven. God cannot be limited. He is everywhere. Nothing can exist beside Him. He does, however, allow his presence to be felt to a greater or lesser degree at certain times, in certain places, to certain people.

4. God created the world by willing it to exist, and He continues to manifest His presence within it. This manifestation is viewed and experienced by humans as God's active micro-management of the world and everything in it. There is no "coincidence" in Jewish belief. Everything that happens in the world is a direct result of His divine intervention.

5. God is just. His justice may seem clear immediately, or it could take thousands of years for the justice of his actions to be revealed.

6. Every person can have a unique, personal relationship with God, regardless of religion, genealogy, or social status. No intermediaries,

either human or angelic, are required.

7. God loves his creations. Without this love the world would cease to exist.

8. God is One. He works alone. No partners, rivals, spouses, or children. Just God.

Torah

Torah is the Hebrew word used to describe the Five Books of Moses. The Torah was given to the Jewish People over 3500 years ago, by God at Mount Sinai and throughout their forty years of wandering in the wilderness, primarily through Moses. It is not a history book, although it contains historical material. It is not a book of stories, although it contains some of the greatest stories ever told. It is the communication of the will of God, and the guide to attaining closeness to the Divine.

Along with the Torah, God taught Moses the interpretations and details behind the laws and commandments of the Torah, as well as the mystical and spiritual secrets hidden within its words. These teachings were transmitted orally by Moses to Joshua and to the elders of the nation. This oral transmission continued from generation to generation until, in the second century of the common era, this Oral Torah began to be written down by the sages, who feared that it would otherwise be forgotten and lost forever. For the next several hundred years the Oral Torah was recorded and edited, resulting in what is called the Talmud. The Talmud contains over two thousand pages of legal discussions and decisions, ethical lessons, mystical teachings, and a wide array of information on topics raging from agriculture to zoology. It continues to be the basis for all Jewish law and ethics, and the primary focus of traditional Torah study.

From the time the Jews received the Torah until their exile to Babylon almost a thousand years later, many prophets communicated the word of God to the people. These prophecies usually exhorted the people to repent, and enumerated the disastrous consequences that awaited them if they didn't. Many of these prophecies also foretold the eventual salvation of the people, and their return to Israel. The recorded prophecies, along with some other divinely inspired books, were canonized as part of the bible, alongside the Five Books of Moses.

(see appendix for the entire list of biblical books)

After the completion of the talmud, various rabbis wrote commentaries to explain and clarify its often abstruse text, and to codify the laws found within it. Many of the same rabbis also wrote commentaries to the books of the bible. In the sixteenth century a Turkish rabbi by the name of Joseph Karo wrote a codification of all of Jewish Law, based on previous codifications, that could be used as a definitive guide and reference for rabbi and learned layman throughout the scattered Jewish communities of the world. He called his code of Jewish law the *Shulchan Aruch*, or "set table", and it became accepted throughout the Jewish world as the definitive guide to Jewish law. It has retained this honor until today.

Since the *Shulchan Aruch,* there have been thousands of commentaries and legal decisions written by rabbis, that are studied alongside the older commentaries to arrive at legal decisions that apply the ancient laws to modern cases.

The overriding principle in Jewish law is that the Torah, both written and oral, is the word of God and therefore, is as applicable today as it was 3,500 years ago. It can be applied to modern circumstances and technology, but it cannot be modified. (See examples of this in the chapter on the Sabbath)

There are 613 commandments, or Mitzvahs, in the Torah. Three hundred and sixty five of them are prohibitions, and two hundred and forty eight are positive actions to perform. An example of a prohibition is, "do not kill". An example of a positive command is, "honor your parents". A large number of the commandments relate to, or are dependent upon, the Jerusalem Temple that was destroyed nearly two thousand years ago, and to the agriculture of the

Land of Israel. Most of these commandments will not be put into full practice until a new temple is built in the Messianic era. The rest of the commandments are split between those relating to interpersonal relationships, those relating to rituals, and those relating to civil and criminal law. Each commandment may contain dozens, or even hundreds, of laws and details that are enumerated in the Talmud and the legal codes. For example, the verse in the Torah says, "when a man shall take a woman", from which the Talmud derives many of the laws relating to the marriage, based on the oral tradition transmitted from Sinai.

Throughout the generations the rabbis added laws to safeguard the original laws of the Torah and to strengthen moral behavior. These rabbinic laws are treated as seriously as the actual Torah laws in the Orthodox community.

The Torah is much more than a law book. It is a guide to life written by the Creator himself. Following His rules and advice enables us to achieve a state of holiness and perfection that connects us to Him, and to fulfill, the true purpose of creation.

BODY, SOUL, AFTERLIFE

Every living thing is made up of two components: the physical and the spiritual. The physical is the body. The spiritual is the life force, or the soul. One cannot exist in this world without the other. Both need to be nourished and cared for. The body needs food, exercise, rest, and shelter. The soul needs the same things, but in spiritual form. The study of Torah, performance of the commandments, and interacting with other living things in a loving and caring manner, provide the soul with all of its needs.

The human soul is on a higher spiritual level than the life forces inhabiting other living things. It is programmed to strive for spirituality and holiness. When a person dies the body is returned to the earth, but the soul moves on to another dimension, referred to in the Talmud as "the world to come". All we know about this world is that it is totally of the spirit and that it is the soul's reward for the positive actions it performed in the physical world. Since the reward is exclusively spiritual, the more spiritually developed the soul, the greater will be it's appreciation and enjoyment of the reward. A soul that has not been spiritually developed will not benefit from the reward of the World to Come, and instead, will find it cumbersome and painful. This pain, caused by a lack of sensitivity and appreciation, is the soul's punishment. In other words, the more engaged the soul was in performing the commandments, prayer, and Torah study, the more spiritually developed and sensitive it will be, and the greater the enjoyment it will experience in the World to Come. A soul that was just used to engage in primarily physical and material pursuits will suffer the pain of not being able to experience the rewards of the World to Come. This is what is commonly referred to as Hell.

Every good action the soul performs during its worldly existence increases its pleasure in the World to Come, and every bad action increases its pain.

According to some mystical teachings it is possible for a soul to be reincarnated into a new body, or even an animal, if it was unable to fulfill its potential in its previous existence. This reincarnation provides the soul the opportunity for *Tikkun*: correcting the faults that prevented it from reaching its full spiritual potential. A person's suffering might actually be a *Tikkun* for something his soul did in a previous life.

One of the fundamental Jewish beliefs is that there will be a resurrection of the dead, at some point following the coming of the Messiah. Exactly how and when this will occur is unknown.

> The explanation that I have offered to describe the soul and the World to Come is just one of many that are accepted in Jewish belief. Other descriptions are more graphic and contain classical "Heaven and Hell" imagery. The bottom line is that no one really knows the truth, as no one has yet offered an eyewitness account.

REWARD AND PUNISHMENT

Every commandment in the Torah has a reward and punishment attached to it. Only a few of them actually state what the reward is. Two examples are, "honoring your parents" and "sending away a mother bird before taking her eggs", both of which promise the reward of "long life" for their fulfillment. The reward for fulfilling the commandments can come in any form, either in this world or in the World to Come. It is actually preferable to receive one's reward in the World to Come, where the reward is eternal.

The punishments for all of the commandments are clearly enumerated, and depend on the severity of the offense. These punishments may be corporal, capital, or monetary in nature and must be administered by an authorized Jewish court of law. For example, the punishment for murder is execution, while the punishment for burglary is monetary. Along with the physical punishments, there are also spiritual ones reserved for the World to Come. With the destruction of the Jerusalem Temple, all capital and corporal punishment ceased to be administered. These punishments, along with all of the rest, are believed to be meted out by God Himself, either in this world or in the World to Come.

There is also reward and punishment for the nation as a whole. The Torah and the prophets describe the terrible punishments that await the Jewish People if they abandon the commandments, and the bountiful rewards if they follow them.

Every person who sins has the opportunity to repent and, thereby, be saved from punishment. This does not apply to sentences decreed by authorized courts, as in the times of the Temple. In those cases the punishment would be applied regardless of the perpetrator's penitence. For example, a murderer would be executed even if he repented. However, where there is no court ordered punishment, repentance does help.

Repentance is a four step process:

1. Recognizing one's sin and accepting responsibility for it

2. Regretting having sinned

3. Concretizing that recognition and regret in a verbal declaration

4.   Committing to never repeat the sin again.

When the sin is perpetrated against another person, one must ask them for forgiveness in order to fully repent. For example, if you insulted someone you must personally approach them and ask them for forgiveness. Without it there can be no repentance.

DIVINE INTERVENTION

Judaism believes that God plays an active role in managing the world, but that He does so within the normal rules of nature that He put into place. This is because He wants people to have the free choice to either believe in Him or not. Were He to openly reveal Himself to the world, this free choice would be negated, since it would be impossible not to believe. Therefore, God "hides" his presence within the world. To those who look for Him, His presence in the world is obvious. To those who choose not to, He remains hidden.

There are times in history when God changes the course of nature to intervene in the world. This intervention is called a miracle. Perhaps the greatest miracle to ever occur was the splitting of the Sea of Reeds, allowing the Jewish People to escape the Egyptian armies during the Exodus. In truth, however, to those who look for God in the world, He is everywhere. Every birth is a miracle. Every sunrise and sunset is miraculous. Life is a miracle. Those who choose not to see God in the world will attempt to scientifically explain even a wondrous event, including the Splitting of the Sea.

Belief in divine intervention leads to a sense of calmness and acceptance. If God controls everything that happens, then whatever happens must be for the best, even though we may not now understand how. If I miss the bus, it must be for the best, for had I been on the bus my life might have taken a turn for the worse.

MESSIAH

The Messiah is a human being, a descendant of King David, who will bring peace and spirituality to the world. He will restore the Jewish People from throughout the diaspora to Israel, rebuild the Temple in Jerusalem, and teach the world about God. For obvious reasons, the Messiah must be alive to fulfill his mission, which is why the Jews cannot accept Jesus. In addition, the requirement of bringing peace to world has not yet been fulfilled either. Jews still await the coming of the Messiah.

According to tradition, the way to hasten the coming of the Messianic Age is through increasing the amount of commandments performed, and by living righteous and benevolent lives. In recent decades a movement within the Orthodox community, based in Israel, has taken upon itself the responsibility to pave the way for the Messiah's arrival by settling the Land of Israel in its' entirety. This group views the modern state of Israel as part the initial Messianic process. This philosophy is, for the most part, espoused by the Modern Orthodox, but rejected by the Ultra Orthodox. The primary reason for their rejection is because the state is not ruled according to Torah law, and because they believe that the Messiah must come before the land is settled.

ISRAEL

According to the bible, God promised the Land of Israel to Abraham, Isaac, and Jacob, as an eternal homeland. Jacob, also called Israel, and his family were forced to leave the land due to famine, and settle in Egypt. Over the next 210 years the Children of Israel suffered in Egyptian bondage until God, through Moses, redeemed them. After forty years of wandering in the wilderness the Israelites, under the leadership of Joshua, returned to their homeland and conquered it. Since then, there have always been Jews living in the Land of Israel.

The Land of Israel maintains a central role in Jewish belief. The majority of the Torah's commandments are based on the Jewish People's ownership of the land. It is considered to be a holy land, without which the nation cannot fulfill its' divine mission and destiny.

Since their exile from Israel, approximately 2000 years ago, the Jews have always prayed and yearned to return to their homeland. A small number succeeded in returning to fulfill the dream, but the overwhelming majority remained in exile. With the founding of the Zionist movement in the late nineteenth century, thousands of Jews began returning to Israel. At that time the land was ruled by the Turks, and then the British. In 1948, the State of Israel was established marking official Jewish sovereignty over the land. Today, after several victories against Arab armies seeking to destroy her, the State of Israel is the flourishing home to over six million Jews, nearly half of the entire world Jewish population. Since Israel's government is not conducted according to Torah law, some Ultra Orthodox Jews deny it's validity, while most simply accept it, and work within it. The Modern Orthodox embrace the state, and see it as a step towards the messianic age. Almost every Orthodox Jew has visited Israel, and many of the younger generation have spent time studying there. While their connection with Israel is great, Orthodox Jews are completely loyal to the countries in which they live.

Rabbi

The title of Rabbi, which literally means teacher, is granted to men upon their completion of a course of study in Jewish law and philosophy that lasts several years. Rabbis serve the community in many different ways including, leading synagogue congregations, teaching in religious schools, serving as religious judges, providing kosher supervision, and presiding over rituals such as weddings and funerals.

Any Jewish male can potentially become a rabbi, assuming that he is religiously observant and can pass the rigorous academic requirements. Rabbis possess no special powers in Jewish law. There is no Jewish ritual that can only be performed by a rabbi. Their only advantage is their knowledge of Jewish law, which is why they are asked to preside over ritual ceremonies. Therefore, all Jewish rituals including weddings, funerals, and bar mitzvahs can be performed without a rabbi. However, since most Jews are not experts at Jewish law, it is highly advisable, and the common practice, to have a rabbi officiate. Divorces and conversions must be performed by qualified experts in Jewish law.

There are no restrictions that apply specifically to rabbis. Rabbis are just regular Jews who have dedicated themselves to studying the Jewish law and custom, and have chosen to serve the community as leaders and teachers.

Gender Equality

Men and women are considered equals in Orthodox Judaism, with the exception of certain legal situations and ritual obligations. The two main legal exceptions are that women cannot serve as judges or witnesses, and they cannot give their husbands a writ of divorce. They can only accept the divorce if he offers it willingly.

The innate differences between the genders are acknowledged, and thus, men and women have different roles when it comes to spiritual practice. Regarding ritual obligations, woman are not obligated in any of the positive commandments that must be performed at, or within, a prescribed time period. This is in order to free the woman's time for her family, and does not imply any lower degree of spiritual potential or status. Woman are, however, obligated in all the prohibitions. For example, a woman is not obligated to pray three times a day, but she is prohibited from eating non-kosher food.

Woman have traditionally shied away from public exposure, and focused on their homes and families. In today's modern society, however, this is usually no longer the case. Many Orthodox women work outside of the home and run all of the household affairs. In most cases they are more eloquent, assertive, educated, and savvy than their husbands. Despite this, they're first priority is always their family.

CONVERTS

Unlike the other major monotheistic religions of the world, Judaism does not endorse proselytizing. The reason for this is simple. Judaism does not claim that it possesses the only legitimate path to spiritual fulfillment. In other words, you don't have to be Jewish to get to heaven.

Judaism teaches a unique, and often rigorous, spiritual path, specific to the Jewish People. There are only two ways to be considered part of the Jewish People: being born of a Jewish mother or converting. Anyone can convert to Judaism, as long as they meet the criteria for conversion. There are three requirements for conversion to Judaism:

1. Males must undergo circumcision.

2. The convert must immerse in a ritual body of water called a *Mikvah.*

3. The convert must study the philosophy and laws of Judaism, and commit to observe all of the laws and commandments. The convert

must also renounce his or her old faith.

The entire conversion process must be done under the supervision of a rabbinic court consisting of three rabbis. If any of the three requirements are not completely fulfilled, the conversion is invalid. Once the conversion is complete, and approved by the rabbinic court, the convert is accepted as a full and equal member of the Jewish People. In fact, Jewish law emphasizes the requirement to treat the convert with extra care and kindness.

Practices

The Sabbath

The Sabbath, or *Shabbos*, is the official Jewish day of rest. It begins at sundown on friday and ends at nightfall on Saturday, every week of the year. The exact time that the Sabbath begins and ends varies according to the time of year, so it is slightly different every week. In the winter months, *Shabbos* can begin as early as 4:00PM, while in the summer, as late as 8:00PM. *Shabbos* ends on Saturday night, about an hour after the time it began. For example, if *Shabbos* begins at 6:00PM, it will end at approximately 7:00PM on Saturday. You can refer to a Jewish calendar for exact weekly times.

Since, according to the Torah, God rested from creation on the seventh day, we too are commanded to refrain from all creative activity. Creative activity has been defined in Jewish law as being any type of productive work or craftsmanship. This includes all the tasks involved in agricultural and construction work, food preparation, and garment production. Some examples of specific tasks included in these broad categories are planting, irrigating, building, writing, repairing, baking, cooking, sifting, grating, sewing, knitting, tearing, and weaving. There are actually thirty nine categories of prohibited acts, which are applied in hundreds of different practical ways. We will just touch on a few that are most noticeable.

Creating or extinguishing a fire, or making a fire larger or smaller, is prohibited on Shabbos. A spark is considered fire. Therefore, any process or activity that results in the creation of a spark or flame, regardless of the effort or exertion required, is prohibited. Using electricity or completing an electric circuit is included in this prohibition. Some examples of common activities and objects that are prohibited on Shabbos include driving a car, turning on a light, using a telephone, TV, computer, using money, writing, conducting any type of business.

Because they cannot use a car on Shabbos, Orthodox Jews must live within walking distance of their synagogue. This is the primary reason why property values rise disproportionately in Orthodox communities.

If you have Orthodox coworkers or employees, be aware that they will not work on Shabbos, no matter how important the job is or how much money is at stake. They will not answer phone calls, emails, or pages until Saturday night. They will leave early on Fridays to be home before Shabbos begins. These rules are not bendable or flexible. The only exceptions are in cases of human life and death, not the death of an account or a company. Medical professionals, firemen, and police officers might have to work on Shabbos. Lawyers, bankers, and accountants will never.

Shabbos is a twenty five hour island of tranquility in an otherwise hectic and stressful week. It is a time for prayer and study, reconnecting with family and friends, catching up on some rest, and wearing your "Sunday finest". It is the much anticipated climax of the Orthodox Jew's week. So next Friday afternoon, when you see your colleague rushing out of the office, wish her a "good shabbos".

Kosher

The laws and regulations relating to food tend to make Orthodox Jews stand out from their non Orthodox friends and coworkers, since they cannot eat with them in regular restaurants, at their homes, or share the food they bring into the office. This can make you, the non Orthodox "outsider", feel insulted, unwelcome, or even unclean. Rest assured, it has nothing to do with you at all. It's all about the food.

Jewish law demands that all food and drink consumed be kosher. The word "kosher" literally means "prepared". In common usage, however, kosher describes any food that may be consumed according to jewish law.

What makes something kosher? Well, it's really quite simple to understand when broken down by categories. Oh, it has absolutely nothing to do with a rabbi blessing the food!

- All produce that grows from the ground is kosher. That includes all fruits, vegetables, grains, and legumes, as long as they are in their raw and unprocessed states. Once they are cooked or processed, their kosher status is no longer guaranteed.

- Fish that have scales and fins are kosher. All other creatures of the water are not. This rule is an explicit verse in the bible! Examples of kosher fish include carp, salmon, and tuna. Non-kosher seafood includes shark, squid, lobster, shrimp, clams, and oysters. Once a kosher fish is cooked or processed, its kosher status is no longer guaranteed.

- Animals that have split hoofs and chew their cud are potential candidates for the kosher butcher. I say potential because in order to be fit for consumption, the animal must be slaughtered and prepared according to strict regulations. For example, if you shoot a kosher animal, it becomes non-kosher. Examples of kosher animals are cows, goats, lamb, deer, and buffalo. Non-kosher animals include camels, horses, dogs, cats, bears, elephants, lions, and of course, pig.

- The Torah offers a long list of species of birds

that are kosher, but most cannot be positively identified by the experts. The ones that are considered kosher include chicken, turkey, goose, duck, and quail. These birds must be slaughtered and prepared in the prescribed manner to be fit for kosher consumption.

● A few species of locust are listed in the Torah as kosher, but the tradition as to their exact identity has been lost. What a relief!

● The milk from a kosher animal is kosher. Therefore, cow's milk is kosher, but camel's milk is not.

When a non-kosher food is cooked together with, or absorbed into, kosher food, the resulting mixture is considered non-kosher. For example, if bread is baked with lard, the bread becomes non-kosher. If oil derived from a non-kosher animal source is cooked with vegetables, the result is a delicious, but non-kosher meal.

When non-kosher food is cooked, the utensils used in the cooking process become non-kosher. If kosher food is then cooked in them, the food becomes non-kosher. For example, if you cook non-kosher meat in a brand new pot, the pot becomes non-kosher. If you then cook salmon (a kosher fish) in that same pot, the salmon becomes non-kosher. If you serve kosher chicken soup in a bowl that was previously used for non-kosher chicken soup, the kosher chicken soup becomes non-kosher. The same applies to ovens, roasters, frying pans, microwaves, plates, bowls, and even forks and knives.

This explains why an Orthodox Jew cannot eat a kosher fish prepared in a non-kosher kitchen. Even if the actual ingredients are kosher, their preparation can make them non-kosher. Therefore, no processed food can be considered to be kosher, without positive proof.

So how do you know if a processed food is kosher? Looking at the ingredients isn't enough, because ingredients comprising less than two percent of the total are not required to be listed, and the status of the utensils used to process the food is unknown. What you need to do, then, is look for the kosher certification on the package. There are scores of organizations that send out kosher inspectors to supervise the processing of food. If they deem the food to be kosher they will, for a fee, allow their identifying logo or symbol to be printed on the package. Some of the well respected US national kosher symbols include the OU, OK, Star-K, and Kof-K. When you see one of these, or any other reliable, logos on the package, you know it's kosher. Some symbols may not be accepted as sufficiently reliable by the Orthodox, so ask them first just to make sure.

There's one more piece to the kosher puzzle: meat and dairy. Meat and dairy may not be cooked or eaten together. That's why you will never find cheesecake on the menu at a kosher steakhouse, or pepperoni on your kosher pizza. No such thing as a kosher cheeseburger! Meat and dairy cannot share the same cooking or eating utensils, which is why all kosher homes have separate sets of each. The law is so strict that you must wait anywhere for three to six hours (depending on family tradition) after eating meat, before eating dairy. Foods that are neither dairy nor meat are called *Parve*, and can be eaten with either.

All drinks must have kosher certification, except for water. Most alcoholic beverages, including beer, whiskey and scotch, are kosher, unless they contain wine or some other non-kosher ingredient. Wine and champagne must be certified kosher. Good kosher wines and champagne can be found in liqueur stores that have kosher customers, but they are usually not found at bars or non-kosher restaurants.

It is important to realize that not all Orthodox Jews hold to the same level of kosher observance. Just because one person might eat a certain food at a certain eatery does not mean that everyone else will. So, if you ask your Orthodox coworker to join you for a salad at a local restaurant and she politely declines, don't say, "well, Sarah ate there, and she's Orthodox!" Just because Sarah did it doesn't mean that it's right, or that other Orthodox people will do it.

Most Orthodox Jews would really love to be able to join you for dinner. They probably feel awkward having to say no all the time, especially when you bring in those homemade cookies that your wife made and you try to convince them that there's nothing non-kosher about them. Stop! Just go have lunch together at a kosher restaurant that Sarah chooses. Remember, it's not personal. It's religion.

Eating

Assuming the food is kosher, there are a few other things that an Orthodox Jew must do before and after eating. Every food has a specific blessing that is recited before eating it. It's just a few hebrew words of thanks to God, that are usually whispered, so you probably won't even notice.

Eating bread, however, requires that one perform a ritual hand washing in addition to the blessing. This hand washing is done by pouring a cup of water over each hand a couple of times and reciting a special blessing. Talking is not permitted between the hand washing and eating. If you try to make conversation with your Orthodox eating partner, he might nod, motion, or make non-verbal sounds, but he won't speak until after taking a bite of bread. It could get really awkward if the table is far from the sink and you insist on hearing the guy's life story, so just wait. It will be appreciated. There's also a blessing recited after eating. The one after bread is long, so be patient.

PRAYER

Orthodox men are obligated to pray three times daily - morning, afternoon, and evening - corresponding to the three daily sacrificial offerings in the Jerusalem Temple of old. The morning service lasts about an half hour, while the afternoon and evening only about 10 to 15 minutes. All the prayers are recited in Hebrew.

The prayers can be recited just about anywhere. The main part of the prayer service is a silent prayer that usually takes a few minutes to recite, during which time the worshiper must stand with his feet together in one place. Many people also sway or rock back and forth during prayer. This practice reflects the idea of using one's entire body to praise God. At several points during the prayer, the worshiper bows from the waist. So, if you see someone standing with their feet together, swaying back and forth, with their lips moving, you can be certain that they are engaged in a highly important conversation with God.

It is preferable to recite the prayers with a

minyan, which is a group of at least ten Jewish men. The minyan usually meets in a synagogue but, if there isn't one available, it can meet anywhere. The usual makeshift minyan venues include conference rooms, private offices, hallways, parking lots, and anywhere else where a group of ten Orthodox Jews find themselves in need of a prayer service. In practice, the afternoon service is usually the only one that is held in these makeshift venues, because it must be recited before sundown, usually right in the middle of the work day.

Unless you are Orthodox, you probably had no idea that there was a prayer service going on during your afternoon coffee break. Well, now you know why your coworker happens to step out for a few moments at exactly the same time every afternoon. Try not to schedule a meeting or decide to pop in and discuss an issue at just that time. You will put him in a tough spot and make him choose between you or God. Who do you think will probably win?

If you happen to pop into your colleague's hotel room bright and early while you're away at that trade convention, you might be shocked to see him wrapped in a white shawl, with black leather straps tied around his head and arm. Don't worry, he's not a pervert or an alien. He's just praying the morning service while wearing the ritual garments required by Jewish law.

The shawl is called a *Talis*. It is white with a few black stripes, and has white strings attached to each of its four corners. It is worn like a cape, and is sometimes draped over the head like a cloak. The *Talis* represents modesty and humility, and the strings, called *Tzitzis*, represent the commandments.

The black leather straps are called *Tfillin*. There are two straps, each attached to a small black box that contains small pieces of parchment with verses from the *Torah* written on them. One box is strapped to the head, just above the forehead, between the eyes. The other is fastened to the left bicep and forearm by wrapping the strap around the arm seven times. Just think of *Tfillin* as a special device that allows one to communicate directly with God.

The *Talis* and *Tfillin* are only worn by men, for the morning service, and are usually packed in an embroidered, blue velvet bag. *Tfillin* are not worn on the Sabbath or Holidays.

Men and women are separated by a *Mechitzah* during prayer services in every Orthodox synagogue.

The *Mechitzah* can be in the form of a balcony, partial wall, lattice partition, or curtain. The purpose of the *Mechitzah* is to help keep the mind of the worshippers focused on the prayers, instead of on the opposite sex. It is not viewed as discriminatory. Many newer Orthodox synagogues have their *Mechitzah* running directly down the middle of the sanctuary, providing both genders with an equal view of the service.

All men and married women must wear a head covering in an Orthodox synagogue. Women should wear skirts reaching below the knee and have their shoulders and cleavage covered. This applies to visitors too. These rules are discussed in detail in the following chapter.

APPEARANCE

The way Orthodox Jews dress, and their general appearance, is based on a combination of Jewish law and custom, which are different for men and women.

Men

Orthodox men are required to have their heads covered at all times, as a constant reminder of God's presence. Any head covering will do, but the one traditionally worn is called the *Yarmulkah* or *Kippah*, or in English, the skullcap. The *Yarmulkah* is usually made of velvet, suede, cloth, or knitted yarn. Most are black or navy, although the knitted ones can be colorful. Some even have patterns or words on them. The knotted *Yarmulkahs* are usually worn by the Modern Orthodox, while the Ultra Orthodox wear black velvet or cloth.

Since wearing a *Yarmulkah* is technically just a custom, if it will be the cause of a large monetary loss, some rabbinic authorities permit not wearing one. For example, some lawyers might not wear a *Yarmulkah* in court for fear of jeopardizing their case, in the event that the judge or one of the members of the jury has some anti-semitic prejudice. Also, there are still, unfortunately, employers that would rather not have a *Yarmulkah* wearing associate or staff member as part of their team. In these cases, many Orthodox men remove their *Yarmulkahs* and go "under cover". Some go bare headed simply not to draw extra attention or make waves, or so as not to be held to a higher standard than the norm. Many men, however, do wear *Yarmulkahs* in their work places. There's no right or wrong here, so you might be in an office with one Orthodox coworker who does wear one and one who doesn't. Asking either of them why they don't do like the other could just make them feel uncomfortable, and create an awkward work environment. Just realize that it's an extremely difficult, and sometimes scary, decision to make, and don't ask.

Since any head covering fulfills the requirement, many orthodox mean wear hats, primarily outdoors. Ultra orthodox men wear black or navy fedoras. Chassidic hats are black, round rimmed, and sometimes made of felt. On the Sabbath, Chassidic men wear large, round, fur hats.

The only specific garment required to be worn by men, according to the Torah, is called *Tzitzis*. It is a four cornered garment, usually white, made from wool or cotton, with strings attached to each corner. The purpose of the garment is to remind the wearer of the commandments. The garment is worn beneath the shirt. Some wear the strings sticking out from beneath their shirts. If you see white strings hanging over your colleagues belt, it's *Tzitzis*.

Modern Orthodox men wear whatever clothing styles everyone else is wearing. Any color or style is acceptable. Ultra Orthodox men primarily wear dress shirts, usually white, with dark slacks. Some wear dark suits or sport jackets, and the fedora. Jeans and tee shirts are strictly for dirty work or outdoor physical activities like football or hiking. Most Chassidic men wear long black coats, regardless of the weather, with black pants and white shirts. They never wear neckties.

Since ancient times, Jews have worn beards. There are two reasons for this, one legal and one mystical. According to Torah law a man is forbidden to run a razor directly against his face. This prohibition might have been a reaction to idolatrous practices, but the reason is really not relevant. The only permitted ways to shave were with a depilatory, or with scissors. A depilatory could burn your face off if not handled properly, and scissors couldn't provide anything close to a shave. Therefore, most men just grew beards. On a mystical level, the beard represents the appearance of holiness, and should not be tampered with. A long, full beard is a sign of honor and piety. Many Chassidic men never cut their beards.

So why are so many Orthodox men today clean shaven? It's thanks to the electric shaver. The blades of an electric shaver do not directly come into contact with the skin. Instead, the hair is held, or in some cases lifted, by one blade and cut by the other, like a scissor. You get a close shave without violating any prohibitions.

One of the areas of the head that cannot be shaved are the sideburns. Technically, the sideburns must extend at least until the middle of the ear. This is the law, followed by all Orthodox men. To make sure this was done properly, the custom became to leave the hair above the sideburns uncut. These side-locks are called "*Payiss*", which literally means corners. Modern Orthodox men and some Ultra Orthodox men do not follow this custom. Many Ultra Orthodox, and all Chassidic, men do. Some have short *Payiss* discretely tucked behind their ears, while some have long flowing *Payiss* that can reach down to their waist. These long *Payiss* are usually hidden beneath a hat during business hours but are set free during prayers and on the Sabbath and holidays. People walk around with dreadlocks, afros, and blue and pink spiked hair, so what's so strange about some holy *Payiss*?

Women

Orthodox women's clothing must conform to standards of modesty laid down by Jewish law. The style and color of the clothing is not regulated, just the amount. Shoulders, upper arms, chest, back, and knees must be covered at all times. There are varying opinions as to the exact lengths and measures required by the law, which are reflected by the fashions worn among different segments of the community. For example, some women will wear skirts that barely cover the knee, while other will insist on skirts that reach the ankles. Some women will wear sleeves that just cover the upper part of the arm, while others will make sure to cover the elbow, and others the entire forearm. Some will wear form fitting clothing, while others only loose fitting. Some will wear bright colors, while others just conservative ones. Ultra Orthodox women do not wear slacks, while some Modern Orthodox do, although never on the Sabbath or holidays. As you can see, there's lots of room for diversity within the legally required framework.

Although women are not required to wear the *Yarlmukah*, married women are required to cover their hair. A woman's hair is considered to possess a sexual quality which must only be shared with her spouse. Women cover their hair with hats, berets, kerchiefs, or wigs. As in any area of Jewish law, there are varying degrees of compliance in the area of hair covering. Many Modern Orthodox women only cover their hair in the synagogue or at other religious venues. Most Ultra Orthodox women exclusively wear wigs, otherwise known as *Sheytels*. Many professional women who work in offices choose to wear *Sheytels* so as not to stand out. These *Sheytels* look exactly like real hair, so there's no way you'll ever be able to tell the difference without some insider information. Not everyone likes, or can afford, to wear a *Sheytel*, so if you see a woman wearing a beret or hat in the office, you now know she's not having a bad hair day or trying to promote the latest Parisian fashion. She's just following Jewish law.

INTER-GENDER ETIQUETTE

All physical contact between men and women outside the context of the marital or familial relationship are prohibited. This rule is primarily to protect against extramarital sexual relationships, as well as to enhance the exclusivity of the marital bond. That means, Orthodox men and women do not touch members of the opposite sex unless it's their spouse or close relative. They do not want to be touched by you, period. That includes casual contact such as tapping and nudging. Hugging and kissing are obviously forbidden. This seems extremely strange in a society where greeting someone with a friendly hug or peck on the cheek is normal, accepted behavior, but it's true. For example, if you're a guy, you can certainly hold the door open for Sarah, but don't place your hand on her back to help her through. If you've just watched your favorite team win a game, don't offer Sarah a "high-five", because she might not respond in kind. If Sarah is looking sad, don't put your arm around her to comfort her even though your heart is pouring out to her in sympathy. It's really not welcome, and could just make matters worse. Trust me on this one. The same applies to woman visa-vi men. So, here's the rule: if they're drowning or falling off a ladder, it's ok to help. Otherwise, don't.

The one area of physical contact that some Orthodox Jews will be flexible in is the handshake. According to some respected Orthodox rabbinic authorities, if a woman offers her hand to a man in a business context, he may shake it so as not to embarrass her. Many Ultra Orthodox do not follow this ruling, and will politely and respectfully refuse the handshake. To be safe, if the person looks Orthodox and is of the opposite sex, don't offer your hand. Let them make the first move.

There are certain places where an Orthodox Jew will probably not feel comfortable. These are the same places where your priest or minister would also not want to be found. Some examples include pick-up bars, discos, gentleman clubs, or any venue that contains lots of scantily clad women. Use your judgement on this one, and be conservative.

EDUCATION

Education has always been a priority in the Jewish family. Stories abound of mothers skimping on food to save up money to send their children to school. In modern times most Orthodox children receive both a secular and religious education in private Jewish elementary and high schools, called Yeshivas. Most Modern Orthodox, and all Ultra Orthodox, communities have separate schools for boys and girls. Orthodox Jews rarely send their children to public schools.

Secular Education

One of the main differences between the Modern and Ultra Orthodox is their attitude towards secular education. The Modern Orthodox whole heartedly espouse secular education at its highest levels, while the Ultra Orthodox accept it as a necessary evil required to fulfill government regulations or to make a decent living. These attitudes manifest themselves in many ways:

- Modern Orthodox schools emphasize excellence in secular studies, offering the highest quality instructors and demanding a high level of achievement from students.

- Ultra Orthodox schools provide just enough secular studies to meet the minimum government educational requirements. Since girls have a lesser degree of obligation regarding religious studies, secular education in girls' schools is taken more seriously and is usually on a much higher standard.

- Almost all Modern Orthodox men and women attend colleges and universities as regular, full-time students. A disproportionate amount attend Ivy League or other first tier schools. Many also attend Yeshivah University in NYC, which combines a traditional, advanced religious studies program with highly respected liberal arts and business colleges.

- Attending college is not the norm in the Ultra Orthodox community, although a significant percentage do attain a college degree by attending non-coed night courses offered by NY based Jewish owned Touro College, or regular night classes at local colleges. Some also attend Yeshivah University or a few other schools that allow them to combine a full day of religious studies and attend college at night. A handful attend regular, liberal arts colleges as full-time students. Many Ultra Orthodox girls continue their post high school religious studies at seminaries in America or Israel for a year or two, and then go to work either as teachers or in the family business. Many men continue their post high school religious studies for several years at Yeshivas in Israel and America and then go on to teach or work in business, without ever attending college. Some attend vocational or technical schools. Some exceptional students manage to get accepted to prestigious law or business schools solely based on their studies at a few high level American Yeshivas.

Religious Education

As stated above, all Orthodox children receive a formal religious education through high school graduation. Almost all Ultra Orthodox and many Modern Orthodox men and women continue their religious education after high school.

It has become the norm for Modern Orthodox men and women to spend their post high school year studying at a Yeshivah (men) or Seminary (women) in Israel before attending college back in the states. Some stay for two years. Upon return, many decide to attend Yeshiva University in NYC, where they can combine Yeshivah study with college. Some men decide to attend Ultra Orthodox Yeshivahs in America and attend college at night, or not at all.

It has also become the norm for Ultra Orthodox men and woman to spend their post high school year at a Yeshiva or Seminary in Israel. Woman usually return after the year to teach, work, or attend vocational school or college, and get married, while men usually remain at Yeshivah, either in Israel or in America, for several more years. Some also attend college, as discussed above.

In general, religious study is considered to be a

lifetime obligation for both men woman. Many adults attend classes and study groups on a weekly or even daily basis. Classes are usually held in the synagogue or Yeshiva, but some are organized in offices or workplaces during lunch hours for the benefit of the busy Orthodox professional.

The Torah scholar is held in the greatest esteem by the community, and acquiring Torah knowledge is seen as a commendable pursuit, even at the expense of leisure pursuits or non critical familial obligations. Primarily in the Ultra Orthodox community some men, almost all married, dedicate many years exclusively to religious study before eventually taking up teaching or Rabbinic positions, or joining the regular workforce.

CHARITY

According to Jewish law a person is obligated to set aside at least ten percent of his or her income for charitable causes. Most Orthodox Jews take this obligation seriously. How exactly the ten percent is calculated, before or after taxes, or whether Yeshiva tuition is included in it is open to interpretation by the legal scholars. However, any way you calculate, it's still a relatively substantial sum of money.

Much of the money goes to support institutions that care for the poor and underprivileged, educational institutions, synagogues, and a myriad of other programs and organizations dedicated to enriching Jewish life. Most of the money stays within the Jewish community, although there are some notable exceptions such as Chabad, that offer their services to the greater non-Jewish community. A substantial amount goes to organizations in Israel and other Jewish communities in need throughout the world.

Wealthy members of the community are often inundated with requests for donations and are, many times, personally approached at their places of business by fundraisers making the rounds of the "known to be" generous.

It is common for members of the community to open their homes to visitors without a place to stay or eat for the Sabbath, or to visit patients in local hospitals or run errands for someone who is bedridden. Helping a fellow member of the community is not seen as a chore, but rather as an opportunity to fulfill God's will. It is truly one of the most beautiful and appealing parts of being part of the Orthodox community.

MEZUZAH

Ever notice a small, rectangular box with Hebrew letters on it, hanging diagonally on the doorpost of your friend's front door? It's not part of the alarm system. It's a Mezuzah. The Mezuzah has become a symbol of good luck and protection, for Jews and non-Jews alike. Many have the custom of touching the mezuzah and then kissing their fingers, as a sign of love and respect.

When God was about to smite the Egyptian firstborns with His tenth and final plague before redeeming the Jews from bondage, He commanded every Jewish household to smear some lamb's blood on their doorposts as a sign for Him to "pass-over" their homes. Therefore, the Torah commands that a Mezuzah be attached to every doorpost of every room in a Jewish home. Some also affix them in offices and stores. The Mezuzah box contains a piece of parchment with a portion of the Torah handwritten on it by a religious scribe.

LIFE-CYCLE

Birth

Having children has always been a fundamental precept in the Jewish community. The birth of a child is not only celebrated by the family, but by the entire community. After all, it is the first commandment in the bible: "Be fruitful and multiply". The six million Jews murdered during the Holocaust has made this commandment even a greater priority to the community. Every newborn is proof of their victory over Hitler and all the other enemies who tried to destroy them.

A newborn girl is officially given her Jewish name in the synagogue, on a day when the Torah scroll is read, usually on the first Sabbath after birth. It's pretty simple. The Rabbi or Cantor recites a special prayer for the speedy recovery of the mother and the child, inserting the name of the child given to him by the father. Mazal Tovs are exchanged and a chorus of a Mazal Tov tune is usually sung, and it's done. Neither the baby nor the mother play any role in the brief ceremony. Of course, there's always a nice spread following services.

A newborn boy gets his Jewish name under much more stressful circumstances. On his eighth day in the world, unless he has medical complications, baby boy becomes a member of the covenant. The Hebrew word for covenant is Bris. How does he enter this holy covenant? You guessed it: circumcision.

In the bible, God commands Abraham to circumcise himself as a covenant between himself and God. God also commands every father to circumcise his son on the eighth day after birth. For the past few thousand years, Jewish fathers have been fulfilling this commandment, usually through the services of a Mohel, or professional circumciser.

Here's what happens. The baby is brought out by the mother and handed to the father or another male relative, who then hands him to the Sahndik, the official baby holder. The Sahndik could be anyone, but the honor is usually given to a close male relative, like grandpa. At this point, the Mohel might offer a few words of explanation and reassure the audience that the baby will feel no pain, since his sensory nerves are not developed yet. Any crying is simply due to all the excitement. Then the Mohel, as the agent of the father, recites a blessing and cuts the baby's foreskin.

The father then recites a blessing and then the Mohel recites a prayer for the child's well-being and proclaims the baby's new Jewish name. Welcome to the covenant! Now that the ceremony is over, there's bagels, lox, whitefish, and some good old scotch, especially for dad.

BAR MITZVAH - BAT MITZVAH

The legal age of maturity according to Jewish law is thirteen for a boy and twelve for a girl. Therefore, on his thirteenth birthday a boy becomes a Bar Mitzvah or "Son of the Commandments", and on her twelfth, a girl becomes a Bat Mitzvah or "Daughter of the Commandments". From that day on, the boy or girl are obligated to fulfill all of the commandments, and are treated as adults in all areas of Jewish law. This change of status occurs automatically, without any ceremonial requirements or rituals, whether the child is aware of it or not.

In recognition of this life changing event it is customary to celebrate it in several special ways. The way we're all probably familiar with is the party. Many of us have read about, or possibly even experienced, the extravagant galas complete with rock bands, dancers, and catered delicacies all centering around a popular theme chosen by the guest of honor. Well, the Orthodox version is much more subtle, although there are always exceptions. In Modern Orthodox communities the Bar Mitzvah and Bat Mitzvah parties will often be of equal magnitude, while in Ultra

Orthodox circles, the Bat Mitzvah party is usually a small, private family affair or simply a hefty spread after the Sabbath morning service in the synagogue.

The second part of the celebration, which usually precedes the party and is viewed as being primary, takes place at Sabbath morning synagogue services, where the Bar Mitzvah boy is called to the Torah to either chant a portion of it or just recite a blessing. Usually, the boy will spend months prior to this learning how to chant the appropriate Torah portion or, if that is too difficult for him, the shorter and easier portion that is read from the Prophets. Many boys would rather jump off a bridge than chant before the congregation, but most get through it unscathed, proud of their achievement and even happier to see the beaming faces of their parents and grandparents. Some boys will also lead part of the service or deliver a short speech at its conclusion. While girls are not called up to the Torah, in Modern Orthodox communities the Bat Mitzvah girl will sometimes speak after services, while in Ultra Orthodox communities the girls do not participate in any part of the synagogue celebration.

The daily life of the newly crowned Bat Mitzvah doesn't really change, although she might be held more strictly accountable by her parents regarding the performance of the commandments. The Bar Mitzvah, however, does feel an immediate change in his daily routine. He is now counted as part of the Minyan, the ten men required for communal prayer services. This can be cause for great pride as well as great inconvenience. The pride comes from the importance of being able to count as a full adult. The inconvenience comes when dad drags you out of bed at 6:00am on a cold, rainy, winter morning to help complete the Minyan.

Another added responsibility the Bar Mitzvah dons is the wrapping of *Tefillin* every morning, except for the Sabbaths and Festivals, at prayers. This means that whenever he goes on an overnight trip or sleep-over, he must bring his *Tefillin* with him. Most young men take their *Tefillin* responsibility seriously and never miss a day.

DATING

Orthodox dating etiquette varies between the modern, ultra, and chassidic segments of the community. The only common denominator is that premarital physical contact is prohibited.

Orthodox Jews will almost always only date other Orthodox Jews. It's not about discrimination, it's about finding someone who shares your beliefs and practices, to build a life together. Of course, there are always exceptions, but if you want to have a kosher home and observe the Sabbath, you need to be with someone who wants the same. Changing your beliefs and lifestyle for someone you love might sound extremely romantic, but it's not realistic, and almost never works. It's just a recipe for heartache and failure, so do yourself a favor and don't try it. If you're not Orthodox, don't attempt to date someone who is, or don't try to fix them up with someone who isn't. Your offer will be politely rebuffed. Even within the Orthodox community there is usually a preference to date within ones particular segment of the community. So just because someone is "religious" doesn't necessarily mean that they will be an appropriate dating partner for your orthodox friend.

Modern Orthodox dating is not much different than good old fashioned American dating. Men and women meet each other at university, parties, social events, through friends or informal matchmakers, or with the help of many online dating websites geared specifically to their particular demographic. Then they date. You know, dinner, drinks, movies, bowling, and all the other fun stuff people do when dating. In most cases, couples will not date longer than a few months before decided to get engaged. Some couples decide sooner and some can date for up to a year. With parental and societal pressures upon them, and with living together not an option, most couples make their decisions as quickly as possible to either get engaged or break up. Engagements usually last no longer than four to six months, just enough time to plan the wedding.

Ultra Orthodox men and women meet exclusively through a matchmaker, who makes the match based on criteria provided by the parents. Criteria may include social and financial status, level of observance, religious education, earning prospects, health considerations, and of course, appearance. Once an appropriate match is made, the couple go out on dates. These will usually be in public places where the couple can talk and get to know each other. After each date, the couple will report back to the matchmaker. If both sides agree, the dating continues. If all goes well, after usually only a few weeks of dating the couple will announce their engagement. In the chassidic community this process is condensed into only one or two dates before the decision is made. At first glance this hasty dating process might seem absurd. However, remember that all the things that usually break up a relationship like cultural, religious, or lifestyle differences, false expectations, incompatible life goals, and interfamily tension are all dealt with by the matchmaker before the match is made. All the couple needs to figure out is if they like each other and can get along. It really doesn't take that long to figure that out. Also, the man and woman have been inculcated with the importance of marrying and building a family from an early age, so when the time comes, they are ready to take the plunge. Divorce rates in the Orthodox community are much lower than among the general population, so the system can't be that bad.

Marriage

The Orthodox wedding, much like all other weddings, consists of a ceremony followed by a catered reception. The bride and groom stand under a wedding canopy, the Chuppah, with the rabbi, their parents, and members of the wedding party. The bride circles the groom seven times. Two male witnesses are called up to witness the groom give the ring to the bride while declaring her his wife. A sip of wine is drunk by the bride and groom, some blessings are recited, the rabbi delivers some words of blessing, more men are called up to recite blessings, and the groom breaks a glass with his heel, signifying our continued mourning for the destroyed Temple in Jerusalem. The crowd then breaks into song as they lead the happy couple away to a private room for a few moments alone.

Prior to the wedding ceremony, some religious documents are signed and witnessed, and the groom is led in a joyous procession of singing and dancing men to greet his bride in a special veiling ceremony called the Badeken. You don't need to memorize all this information. Just ask anyone at the wedding and they'll be more than happy to explain everything.

The dancing at the reception is done in large circles to lively Jewish music and is separated by gender. That means, men dance with men and women with women, but like I said, it's not one on one dancing, so you won't feel too strange. Just place your hands on the shoulder of the guy or gal in front of you and go with the flow!

Mazal Tov!

DEATH

The Jewish laws relating to death and mourning focus on respecting the deceased and comforting the living.

Other than in extenuating circumstances, the funeral and burial must take place as soon as possible after death, usually the next day. Autopsies are forbidden, unless they can lead to saving someone else's life. The deceased is washed and clothed in plain white garments by specially trained community members, and placed in a simple wooden coffin. The coffin is present at the funeral, but remains closed. After the funeral, which is composed of prayers and eulogies, the coffin is carried out of the funeral home, and followed by the mourners and the congregation. At the cemetery, some prayers are recited and the coffin is placed in the grave. The mourners each take turns filling the grave with some earth, and then the immediate family members walk through two rows of mourners who offer words of comfort as they leave.

The mourning family returns to one of their homes, where they will spend the next seven days sitting on low stools, mourning their loss. This seven day period is called the *Shiva*. During the *Shiva,* people come to the house to comfort the mourners. It is customary not to begin conversation with the mourner, but to wait until they begin. The purpose of the visitors is not to cheer up the mourners or to take their mind off of their loss. It is to show the mourners that they are not alone and to give them the opportunity to talk and reminisce about their dearly departed. It is not customary to bring gifts or flowers to the house of mourning.

Only sons, daughters, spouses, parents, and siblings are required to observe the *Shiva*. It is customary for them to remain at home for the entire seven days, except for the Sabbath. Prayer services are held in the home. The Orthodox community makes great effort to comfort their members in mourning. *Shiva* homes are usually full of concerned friends and visitors. These visits play a very important role in helping the mourners get through the difficult period of initial loss.

After the Shiva there is an additional twenty three day period of less intense mourning. During this second period, the mourners may not shave or take haircuts, listen to music, or participate in social events. The rules relating to music and social events apply for the entire year to a son or daughter mourning a parent.

HOLIDAYS

CALENDAR

The Hebrew calendar is based on the lunar cycle, with an extra month added every few years to make sure that Passover always falls in the beginning of spring. Every new moon marks the beginning of a new month.

The day, in Jewish law, begins in the evening. The week has seven days, with the Sabbath being the seventh. Sunday, or actually Saturday night, is the first day of the week.

The dates of the Jewish holidays are set according to the Hebrew calendar and, therefore, do not fall on the same secular date every year. For example, the secular new year is always on Jan. 1, while the Jewish new year, Rosh Hashanah, falls on the first day of the hebrew month of Tishrei, usually sometime in September or early October.

There are major Jewish holidays, and not so major ones. On the major ones, all work is prohibited and all the Sabbath laws apply. The not so major ones carry no work prohibitions.

The major holidays are:

    1.   Rosh Hashanah

    2.   Yom Kippur

    3.   Sukkes

    4.   Passover

    5.   Shevu-ehs

The not so major ones are:

    1.   Chanukah

    2.   Tu Bishvat

    3.   Purim

    4.   Lag Bomer

    5.   Tisha Bav

There are also several fast days during the year besides the ones included in the holidays. It's pretty easy to find a Jewish calendar on the internet, if you want to keep track of the current dates. For a complete chart of the holidays, see appendix, pg. 101.

ROSH HASHANAH

Rosh Hashanah is the Jewish New Year and the Day of Judgement for the entire world. This holiday usually falls during September and lasts for two days. All the Sabbath prohibitions apply.

On Rosh Hashanah, at least the first half of each day is spent in the synagogue. The highlight of the service is the blowing of the ram's horn, or Shofar. The Shofar represents Man's cry to God for mercy.

It is both a solemn time of introspection and prayer, since it is the Day of Judgement, as well as a joyous holiday, since there is optimism that the verdict will be favorable. Families join in festive meals for dinner and lunch on both days.

The day following Rosh Hashanah is a fast day. The fast lasts from dawn until sunset. The week following Rosh Hashanah is a time of repentance, leading into Yom Kippur.

YOM KIPPUR

Yom Kippur is the Day of Atonement, when Jews ask, and hopefully receive, forgiveness for their sins. It falls exactly ten days after the first day of Rosh Hashanah and lasts one day. The day is primarily spent in the synagogue. All of the Sabbath prohibitions apply, and eating, drinking, and wearing leather shoes is prohibited. That's why you see men in suits and sneakers.

It is customary for people to ask each other for forgiveness before the holiday. The completion of Yom kippur is usually marked by a break-fast after nightfall.

Sukkes (soo-kes)

The holiday of Sukkes falls five days after Yom Kippur and lasts for eight days. It is named for the Sukkah, a hut that Orthodox Jews eat their meals in during the holiday, to remember the huts that the Jews lived in during their forty years of wanderings in the wilderness, and the protection that God bestowed upon them. The Sabbath prohibitions apply to the first two days and the last day of Sukkes. Therefore, no going into the office on those days.

During the morning prayer services throughout the holiday, except on the Sabbath, a lulav and esrog are held and shaken. The lulav is a long, green, palm branch and the esrog is a fruit that looks like a bumpy lemon. These, along with two other species of flora, represent different aspects of a person's personality and soul, which come together to serve God. It's a very mystical experience to watch hundreds of men waving their lulav and esrogs in unison in synagogue. You might see Orthodox Jews carrying these flora in the street on their way to synagogue.

Men are required to eat all meals in the Sukkah.

Drinks, fruit, vegetables, non wheat based snacks and candy, are permitted outside the Sukkah. Any food made from wheat must be eaten in the Sukkah. Examples of foods that must be eaten in a Sukkah include bread, sandwiches, pasta, quiche, cookies, and cake. Women are not obligated to eat in a Sukkah, although many make an effort to, when possible. Eating in the Sukkah is not required in inclement weather.

The Sukkah must be constructed according to specific regulations outlined in Jewish law. Not every "hut" is considered a Sukkah. Your Orthodox friend will know where to find a real one.

SIMCHAS TORAH

The day after the eighth day of Sukkes is the holiday of Simchas Torah, the celebration of the Torah. This holiday lasts for one day and contains all the Sabbath prohibitions. Every Sabbath in the synagogue, one portion of the Torah is read. It takes one year to complete the reading of the entire Torah. Simchas Torah commemorates that completion.

The highlight of Simchas Torah is the dancing with the Torah scrolls in the synagogue. The celebrations happen at night and during the day, and alcohol is plentiful. Sometimes the celebrations even spill into the streets.

Chanukah

The holiday of Chanukah usually falls in December and lasts for eight days. Each day one additional candle is lit on the Menorah, the ritual candelabra. The holiday commemorates two miracles that took place over 2000 years ago in Israel. In around 135 BCE the Syrian-Greek empire ruled Israel and outlawed Jewish religious observance. The Jews, led by Judah Maccabee and his brothers, rebelled and succeeded in driving their numerically superior enemies out of the country. This was the first miracle.

When the Jews returned to purify their Temple in Jerusalem they could only find one tiny flask of oil that had not been defiled, with which to light the Menorah, which was supposed to remain constantly lit. This tiny flask of oil was enough to burn for only one day. Miraculously, the oil burned for eight days, until a new supply of purified oil could be supplied.

Chanukah is a joyous holiday representing light and freedom. It is celebrated with parties, gifts, and oily foods such as potato *latkes* (pancakes) and jelly doughnuts. No prohibitions are specific to Chanukah.

Purim

The joyous holiday of Purim commemorates the rescue of the Jews from destruction in the Persian empire, over 2500 years ago. The story is as follows. In a fit of drunken anger, Persian king Ahashverosh has his queen executed. He then holds a kingdom wide beauty contest to choose a new queen. A young Jewish girl by the name of Ester wins and becomes queen, but does not reveal her Jewish identity. Meanwhile, Haman, the royal prime minister, convinces the king to wipe out every Jew in the 127 provinces of his kingdom, for no particular reason other than anti semitism and the promise of looting their possessions. Mordechai, a Jewish member of the royal court and Ester's uncle, gets wind of the plot and tells Ester to intervene with the king, at the risk of her own life. To make a long story short, Ester reveals her Jewish identity and succeeds in persuading the king not to destroy her people, but instead, to hang Haman and his cabal. The day on which the Jews were to be destroyed is turned into a day of celebration: Purim. The day preceding Purim is a fast day named after Ester, commemorating her plea for all the Jews fast and pray for the success of her mission.

Purim usually falls in March and lasts for one day. On the night of Purim, immediately following the conclusion of the Fast of Ester, a scroll containing the entire Purim story, called the Megillah of Ester, is read in Synagogue. The Megillah is also read the next morning. Every time the name of Haman is read, it is drowned out by the sound of noisemakers called *Grahgers*, usually wielded by children.

The ancient custom is to wear masks and costumes, exchange gifts of food, give charity, and partake in a festive meal. It's also customary to get drunk!

Although there are no prohibitions attached to the holiday, most Orthodox Jews will take the day off from work to celebrate, if possible.

PASSOVER

The holiday of Passover falls at the beginning of spring, usually April, exactly thirty days after Purim, and lasts for eight days. Passover, or *Pesach*, commemorates the redemption of the Jews, led by Moses, from Egyptian bondage almost 3500 years ago. The Sabbath prohibitions apply to the first two and last two days of the holiday.

On the first two nights, families gather to take part in the Seder. The Seder is much more than a delicious meal with special passover foods. It is an interactive educational experience meant to teach the children, and the adults, the story and lessons of the Exodus. The main text recited at the Seder is the Haggadah. Four cups of wine are drunk to represent freedom, bitter herbs are eaten to represent slavery, and of course, there is Matzah, representing both freedom and slavery.

What is Matzah, and why is it eaten on Passover? The Torah tells us that when God took the Jews out of Egypt it was so sudden that they didn't even have enough time to allow their dough to rise, or leaven. Therefore, all they had was unleavened bread, known as Matzah.

The Torah forbids the consumption or ownership of all leavened products on Passover. Anything made with flour and water will begin to rise if left alone. The dough used to make Matzah must be completely baked within eighteen minutes of its kneading. The Matzah making process is strictly supervised to ensure that the Matzah is fit for passover consumption. Any food that contains flour and water is forbidden to be owned or eaten on Passover, unless it was specifically made with Matzah. Kosher for Passover foods will often be made with potato flour or other grain substitutes. In addition, Jews of European ancestry are prohibited from eating corn, rice, and most beans. It is quite challenging.

The only way to know if a food is Kosher for Passover is to look at the label for an appropriate Kosher for Passover certification. The only items that do not need special certification are raw fruits and vegetables, and water. Since foods that are not Kosher for Passover are considered to be non kosher for the duration of the holiday, separate dishes and utensils must be used for Passover. All Orthodox homes have separate dishes and kitchenware for

Passover. Not all kosher restaurants will be open for Passover, so make sure to find out in advance before scheduling a meeting at one.

Omer

The *Omer* is the period of forty nine days between the second day of Passover and the holiday of *Shavuos* (see next chapter). Each day is counted by reciting a special blessing. The counting commemorates the time between the barley harvest, represented by the barley offering, which weighed an *Omer* (a biblical measure), that was brought to the ancient Temple in Jerusalem, and the first wheat offering that was brought forty nine days later.

The *Omer* period was a joyous time in ancient Israel until the second century CE, when 24,000 students of the sage Rabbi Akiva died suddenly during thirty three of these forty nine days. The Talmud claimed these deaths as punishment for the students' disrespect towards each other, and proclaimed thirty three days of semi mourning during the *Omer*. To add to the sadness, entire Jewish communities were massacred by crusader armies during this period in the Middle Ages.

Therefore, the custom is to refrain from getting married, listening to live music, getting haircuts, or shaving during the *Omer*. Since it is a custom, and not a law, if it will jeopardize his job, a man may shave. According to some customs, shaving is permitted for any reason.

The thirty third day of the *Omer* is called *Lag B'ome*r and is commemorated as the day when Rabbi Akiva's students stopped dying. Many weddings are traditionally held on *Lag B'omer*.

Sʜᴀᴠᴜᴏs

The holiday of *Shavuos*, which literally means weeks, falls the day after the seven weeks of the *Omer*, seven weeks after Passover, and lasts for two days. The Sabbath prohibitions apply.

Shavuos is the day when the Jews received the Torah at Mt. Sinai over 3,500 years ago. To commemorate this event, the custom is for Orthodox Jews to study the Torah the entire first night of the holiday, until dawn.

Shavuos also commemorates the wheat harvest in Israel, and many synagogues are decorated with greenery to represent God's bounty. Dairy products are traditionally eaten during the holiday.

TISHA B'AV

Tisha B'av, the ninth day of the Hebrew month of Av, is the saddest day of the Jewish year. It is the day when both the first and second Jerusalem Temples were destroyed. Many other tragic events throughout Jewish history also occurred on this day.

Tisha B'av usually falls in August and lasts one day. Eating, drinking, and wearing leather shoes are prohibited. Men and women sit on the floor or on low stools, like mourners, and recite lamentations over the tragedies and destructions, at evening and morning synagogue services. The custom is not to greet one another. All entertainment and celebration is forbidden. Although it is not prohibited to work on *Tisha B'av*, many will take the day off to fast and mourn.

The three weeks preceding Tisha B'av, beginning with the fast of the 17th of *Tammuz*, are also days of mourning for the destruction of Jerusalem. The *Omer* customs apply (see pg.95).

PJ Library, org

APPENDIX

Sharkbot Shalom

List of Holidays

Holiday	Days	Approx. Month	Reason	Work Prohibited	Pg.
Rosh Hashanah	2	September	New Year/ Judgement	Yes	84
Yom Kippur	1	Sept. - Oct.	Day of Atonement	Yes	85
Sukkes	8	October	Huts in wilderness	1st 2 and last days	86
Simchas Torah	1	October	Torah completed	Yes	88
Chanukah	8	Nov. - Dec.	Miracle of Lights	No	89
Tu Bishvat	1	Jan. - Feb.	Tree New Yr.	No	
Purim	1	Feb. - March	Salvation in Persia	No	90
Passover	8	April	Exodus from Egypt	1st 2 & last 2 days	92
Lag B'Omer	1	May	Dying ceased	No	95
Shavuos	2	May-June	receive Torah	Yes	97
Tisha B'Av	1	July-Aug.	Temple Destruction	No	99

List of Fast Days

Fast of	Approx. Month	Commemorates
Gedalia	Day after Rosh Hashanah	Assassination of Jewish leader
Tenth of Tevet	December	Beginning of Jerusalem siege
Esther	Day before Purim	Fasting for Esther's mission
Seventeenth of Tammuz	July	Breaking the walls of Jerusalem
Tisha B'Av	July-Aug.	Destruction of Temples
Yom Kippur	Sept. - Oct.	Day of Atonement

The Books of the Hebrew Bible
(in English and Hebrew)

The Five Books of Moses
Genesis - Bereshit
Exodus - Shmot
Leviticus - Vayikra
Numbers - Bamidbar
Deuteronomy - Devarim

The Prophets – Neviim	
Joshua – Yehoshua	Hoshea
Judges - Shoftim	Yoel
Samuel 1 - Shmuel 1	Amos
Samuel 2 - Shmuel 2	Obadiah
Kings 1 - Melachim 1	Jonah
Kings 2 - Melachim 2	Micah
Isaiah - Yeshayahu	Nahum
Jeremiah - Yirmiyahu	Habakkuk
Ezekiel - Yichezkel	Zephaniah
	Haggai
	Zechariah
	Malachi

The Writings - Ketuvim	
Ruth, Esther	Daniel
Ecclesiastes - Kohelet	Ezra
Song of Songs - Shir Hashirim	Nehemia
Lamentations – Eichah	Job - Iyov
Chronicles 1 - Divrei Hayamim	Psalms - Tehillim
1 Chronicles 2 - Divrei Hayamim 2	Proverbs - Mishley

Historical Timeline

(BCE = Before Common Era   CE = After Common Era)

1812 BCE   Patriarch Abraham is born.

1428 BCE   Israelites enslaved in Egypt.

1312 BCE   Moses leads Jews out of Egypt.

1312 BCE   Jews receive the Torah at Mt. Sinai.

1272 BCE   Jews conquer Canaan (Israel).

877 BCE   King David reigns over Israel.

836 BCE   King Solomon reigns.

825 BCE   First Holy Temple in Jerusalem built.

586 BCE   Temple destroyed by Babylonians. Jews exiled.

370 BCE   Jews return from exile.

355 BCE   Miracle of Purim.

352 BCE   Second Holy Temple in Jerusalem built.

139 BCE   Miracle of Chanukah.

63 BCE   Rome conquers Israel.

67 CE   Israel revolts against Rome.

70 CE   Romans destroy Temple. Over a million Jews killed or enslaved.

312 CE   Rome converts to Christianity. Persecution against Jews begins. Jews settle throughout Western Europe, the Middle East, and Asia minor.

1096 CE   Crusades begin. Jews are massacred throughout Germany and France.

1492 CE   Jews are expelled from Spain.

1567 CE   Jews are invited to settle in Poland.

1648 CE   Cossacks massacre over a hundred thousand Jews in Eastern Europe.

1654 CE   First Jews arrive in America.

1698 CE   Chassidic movement founded.

1791 CE   Emancipation of Jews begins in Western Europe.

1810 CE   Reform Judaism founded in Germany.

1882 CE   Jews begin returning to Israel - 1st Aliyah.

1887 CE   Conservative Judaism founded in America.

1933 CE   Hitler gains power in Germany.

1939 CE   World War Two begins. During the next 6 years, 6 million Jews are murdered by Nazis their allies.

1947 CE   Palestine partitioned by UN into Jewish and Arab states.

1948 CE   Israel declares independence. Arab nations attack and are defeated.

1967 CE   Israel defeats Arab armies in 6 days, and reunifies Jerusalem as Israel's capital.

1973 CE   Syria and Egypt attack Israel on Yom Kippur. Israel defeats them.

1979 CE   Israel and Egypt sign peace treaty. Israel gives the Sinai peninsula to Egypt.

1994 CE   Israel and Jordan sign peace treaty.

2008 CE   Israel and the Jewish people survive!!

MORE FROM RABBI ARNIE SINGER

Deep Waters
Insights into the Five Books of Moses and the Jewish Festivals.

Torah is the Hebrew word used to describe the five books of Moses, known to the Christian world as the Old Testament. The Torah was given to the Jewish People by God at Mount Sinai and throughout their forty years of wandering in the wilderness. It is not a history book, although it contains historical material. It is not a book of stories, although it contains some of the greatest stories ever told. It is the communication of the will of God, and the guide to attaining closeness to the Divine.
Deep Waters reveals some of the lessons and messages of the Torah and the Jewish festivals, and applies them to our modern day lives.

To order: www.arniesinger.com

Soulencounter (Music CD)
Rabbi Arnie sings the Friday night Kabbalat Shabbat service along with several original compositions on spiritual themes.

To order: www.arniesinger.com

1532661R00066

Made in the USA
San Bernardino, CA
27 December 2012